Original title:
Echoes Through the Hallways

Copyright © 2025 Creative Arts Management OÜ
All rights reserved.

Author: Derek Caldwell
ISBN HARDBACK: 978-1-80587-059-3
ISBN PAPERBACK: 978-1-80587-529-1

Lyrics of the Forgotten Realms

In the kingdom of odd socks, they dance all night,
With mismatched slippers, oh what a sight!
The prince is a jester with a crown made of cheese,
While the knights borrow steeds from the bees.

A dragon in pajamas chases a cat,
Who steals all the gold while wearing a hat.
The wizard's all tangled in bubblegum spells,
Casting laughter as charm when the village repels.

In the castle of giggles, the walls wear a grin,
With cauldrons of soup that are bubbling with sin.
The goblins play tag with a magical broom,
While the princess is lost in a musical room.

The clock strikes a dance, and the walls start to sway,
As the portly old troll steals the show in ballet.
With sprinkles of joy in the air oh so grand,
In this realm of the silly, we all take a stand.

Halls Bathed in Nostalgia

In corners where the laughter grows,
Old sneakers squeak and dance like prose.
The lockers creak with secrets shared,
While gum under benches shows we dared.

Ghosts of lunchboxes, mismatched socks,
A history tucked in aging clocks.
There's a whiff of fries, a hint of fun,
As we chase our dreams, one by one.

The Unwritten Stories on the Walls

Each scratch and mark, a tale unfolds,
Of mysteries in a world so bold.
A heart carved deep, a smile so sly,
The janitor's frown, at all that can fly.

Doodles of aliens, monsters, and more,
An epic saga, behind every door.
The paint peels back, a canvas to see,
Of chalkboard battles 'tween you and me.

Soundwaves of Silence

Whispers float like butterflies,
In hallways where the laughter lies.
A sneeze erupts, and heads all turn,
The giggles spark, and hearts will burn.

The tiptoe dance, a curious feat,
As we dodge the teacher's stern retreat.
In moments still, the shout rings clear,
In empty rooms, we hold our cheer.

The Quiet Dance of Timeworn Spaces

The floorboards creak a timeless tune,
While shadows prance beneath the moon.
A locker slams, a shoe gets tossed,
In memory's grip, we're never lost.

The whispers of history sway and glide,
As we trip on dreams we dare to hide.
With each old frame, a grin we wear,
For in these halls, we float on air.

Solstice of Silence

In the hall where shadows play,
A sock was lost, who knows the way?
The cat just laughed, took off with glee,
While I yell 'Hey! Come back to me!'

The clock ticks loud, like it's a race,
But all that's here is a silly face.
A joke is whispered in the breeze,
While I dance around like a clown on knees.

Memory Lane in the Twilight

Down the path of thoughts long gone,
I tripped and fell—oh, what a yawn!
A sandwich lost, the dog did scheme,
He ate my lunch—I had to scream!

The streetlights flicker, like they're shy,
I wave at ghosts, they wave back—my!
A tumbleweed, a rogue old hat,
Rolls down the lane, must be a cat!

The Chorus of Faded Voices

Whispers dance upon the air,
It seems they're poking fun, I swear!
The walls all giggle, they know my name,
A hallway war, but who's to blame?

Old memories lean and creak in time,
Mixing up the punchline rhyme.
A parrot shrieks, it cracks a pun,
While I just stand here, holding fun!

Darkness at Dawn

When morning breaks, I clutch my tea,
Stumbling 'round as silly as can be.
The curtains peek, they poke their head,
While I chase ghosts that tease my bed.

A sleepy cat, with one eye closed,
Steals my seat, oh the joy of woes!
I step on toys, a landmine zone,
And in my heart, I still feel home.

A Symphony of Solitude

In the quiet, I hear a tune,
A sock that dances, all alone, too soon.
The cat conducts with paws in flight,
As walls hum softly, a silly sight.

A chair creaks out, it's joining in,
While the fridge hums like it's lost in sin.
Chairs start a jig on swirling floors,
And dust bunnies sway, opening doors.

Footsteps patter like tap shoes bright,
As shadows sway under the moonlight.
Laughter bounces from corner to edge,
While I sip tea from my favorite wedge.

In solitude's embrace, oh what a show,
Plays unseen, there's always a glow.
With each little sound, I giggle and play,
Creating my ballet in a peculiar way.

Flickers of Light in Forgotten Places

In the attic, a light bulb blinks,
A ghostly wink that surely thinks.
Old boxes groan like tired gnomes,
While dust bunnies nest in their cozy homes.

The clock ticks slowly, a jester's tune,
Creaking wood like a bright full moon.
A shadow jumps, a friendly fright,
As I dance with ghosts, oh what a sight!

Beneath the stairs, a spider spins,
Threads of laughter and playful sins.
The floors vibrate with giggly sounds,
As memories spring like lost playgrounds.

A picture falls, but it won't break,
Just grins at me, what a silly cake!
Old memories sparkle, like firefly trails,
Lighting up tales where laughter prevails.

The Breath of Yesterday

In the hallway, whispers shared,
Laughter lingers, adventures dared.
Old shoes shuffle to a forgotten beat,
As the past dances on tiny feet.

A mirror chuckles at the sight,
Reflecting all the wrongs and rights.
It holds the secrets of days gone by,
With every glance, it gives a shy sigh.

Once upon a time, a cat did prance,
Chasing ghosts in a whimsical dance.
And dusty portraits with silly grins,
Remind me of all my childhood sins.

The walls can laugh if you listen close,
With tales of fun, they're better than prose.
In the echoes of right now and then,
The breath of yesterday hums again.

Echoes of Familiar Strangers

In the noise of a crowded room,
Silly faces, like flowers in bloom.
A wink here, a nod just for fun,
As strangers become acquaintances on the run.

The ice cream truck plays a catchy tune,
While a dog barks back, thinking it's June.
We swap stories, tales of delight,
Like puzzle pieces in a dance at night.

Familiarity blooms like wildflowers bright,
As confessions float in the soft twilight.
Each chuckle a door that opens wide,
With laughter and joy that we can't hide.

In this clamor, a symphony rings,
The humor of life in all of its flings.
So let's dance through the laughter we find,
In the echoes of strangers, together we bind.

The Halls of Memory

In the halls where laughter roams,
I trip on thoughts like wayward gnomes.
A pizza slice flies past my head,
Saying, 'Find another place to tread!'

The echoes of my youthful pranks,
Swinging from my childhood banks.
With every turn, a memory stirs,
As I dodge my friends and their snowy furs.

A game of tag, where I am 'it',
Running in circles, just won't quit.
But then I fall, my hands go down,
And suddenly, I'm the laughter clown!

So here I stand, a fool to see,
In these halls, I feel so free.
Though time may roll, I can't resist,
Chasing laughter, in a funny mist.

Reflections in the Gloom

In corners where shadows seem to dance,
I sparked a light, took a silly chance.
The mirror laughed, what a funny sight,
A sleepy snack with socks on tight!

Through whispers of the folks long gone,
Their jokes float by, like a playful song.
They shout, 'Remember when you tripped?'
I raise my hands, the coffee sipped!

The gloom can't dim a silly thought,
Of mishaps and blunders that I have brought.
The ghosts around are rolling on floors,
Telling tales of the mighty who snore.

So I laugh with spirits of old,
In reflections somehow retold.
They're saying, 'Join us, it's quite a spree!'
With laughter echoing, it's all so free!

Lingering Voices of Yesteryear

In the corners where echoes hang,
I hear a voice, it starts to sang.
'Remember me with that big blue hat?'
Oh please, just spare me much of that!

With every step, a tale unfolds,
Of wild escapades and crazy molds.
I can hear them whisper, 'Where's the cake?'
They're hungry for laughter, for goodness' sake.

The tales get wilder as we to roam,
In past's embrace, I find a home.
No one's shy to bring up the past,
Echoing giggles that always last.

So join me now in this memory spree,
Of sassy fables shared like tea.
For voices linger with every cheer,
Of yesteryear's mischief, full of beer!

Haunting Melodies of Time

A tune plays softly in the mist,
Of antics past, it's hard to resist.
Can you feel the rhythm of fate?
Dancing with chairs, oh, isn't it great?

I twirl around like I own the show,
But trip on my shoelace, oh no, oh no!
The notes echo with laughter so bright,
As I swing my arms and take flight.

Melodies call, with playful tease,
As I try to tap dance, oh please!
Ghosts of rhythm join the rhyme,
Swaying to the beat, lost in time.

So gather 'round for this silly show,
With hauntings softer than fresh fallen snow.
In melodies sweet, I hear the chime,
Of laughter ringing, a funny rhyme!

Murmurs Behind Closed Doors

Whispers tickle like a breeze,
Rumors dance on sneezy knees.
Laughter spills from every seam,
Secrets shared, a jolly dream.

Pots are clanging, mice do scamper,
Old grandpa's snoring, what a tamper!
The cat's a thief, a furry ghost,
Stealing snacks, it grins the most.

Beneath the stairs, a party brews,
Old socks waltz in mismatched shoes.
With a whoop, they stomp and twirl,
While curtains sway in a lively whirl.

Footsteps on Ancient Stone

Clatter echoes, what a sight,
Old boots bounce with sheer delight.
A tap dance starts, the stones arise,
Ghostly feet in a comical guise.

Slippery tiles, a prankster's glee,
Someone slips—oh dear me, me!
With giggles swirling 'round the bend,
Footsteps score a laughter blend.

Tales of knights and ladies prance,
While dust bunnies take a chance.
With every stomp, a history told,
As laughter gains, the night unfolds.

Silent Reverberations

Whispers trapped in sleepy nooks,
They tumble out like clumsy books.
Pages flutter, tales rewind,
A sarcophagus of the mind.

Jokes of yesteryears emerge,
Like misplaced socks, they dance and surge.
In quiet corners, giggles wait,
Stretched out, they simply celebrate.

The spoon's a ladle, what a shock!
Chairs may rock without a clock.
In musty air, an old pun sways,
Tickling senses in funny ways.

Ghosts of the Past Linger

Phantom friends with silly charms,
Waltz through walls with cheeky arms.
They drop a wink, glide with flair,
In every creak, surprise is there.

Mirthful moans, a chuckling breeze,
With every sweep, they tease and tease.
Banana peels on marble floors,
Watch out for those ghostly scores!

Yet, here they linger, sly and coy,
As we recount the fun with joy.
In hidden corners, laughter glows,
In the heart of where the mystery grows.

The Weight of Echoing Nostalgia

In corners where old laughter spun,
A shoe squeaks, is that a pun?
The whispers paint tales in a haze,
Of silly pranks from bygone days.

Forgotten snacks beneath the chair,
Old gum that's stuck, a biohazard dare.
The tickle of dust on noses brings,
Resounding notes of forgotten swings.

A portrait grins, its eyes go wide,
It's watching all, no place to hide.
As shadows dance in goofy threads,
And chuckles fill the cracks instead.

With memories wrapped in cotton candy,
This house knows fun—oh so randy!
It sings a tune of playful glee,
A symphony of light-hearted spree.

Soliloquies of Solitude

In silence, the chair creaks a tune,
An old cat stretches, but not too soon.
The clock ticks with a sarcastic flair,
While dust bunnies plot in midair.

The fridge hums jokes, all cheesy delight,
Guarding pickles at the edge of night.
The lone sock dances, it knows no bounds,
As laughter hides in playful sounds.

The echo of feet on a tile parade,
Makes ducks waddle in a quirky charade.
It's a solo act—pantomime of fun,
With walls chuckling, the night's begun.

In the solitude, silliness reigns,
Where the light flickers and the humor gains.
A soliloquy of giggles galore,
For hidden moments and laughs evermore.

The Dusty Diary of Halls

In dusty nooks where giggles hide,
A diary waits, full of snide.
With scribbles of pranks and bumbles galore,
It tells of mischief and so much more.

Oh, the antics of Bert and his pie,
It flew high—up to the sky!
While Sally snorted as she tried to read,
Stumbling through each laughter-filled deed.

Leftover confetti from a wild surprise,
A memory wrapped in glittery ties.
The halls remember every whim and jest,
As echoes of laughter pulse through the rest.

Dear diary, how you chatter and sigh,
With secrets kept and a winked eye.
Each page a memento to cherish and share,
In the dusty corners, joy fills the air.

When Walls Remember

When walls sigh, they chuckle too,
Recalling the days when pranks grew true.
A shoe thrown right, it missed by a mile,
And made the whole room break into a smile.

A ghostly dance in the twilight glow,
Is that a spook? No, just Joe's toe!
The corners whisper with playful cheer,
As echoes grin, our friends draw near.

A tickle from the cobwebbed air,
Makes everyone jump, without a care.
The wallpaper peels with a cheeky gleam,
And the paint joins in on the funny theme.

When walls remember, they start to play,
With each little memory, spinning a sway.
So let us laugh in this jovial domain,
For every chuckle, we're never plain.

Shadows Speak in Elegy

In corners dark, they laugh and play,
Mismatched socks find their own ballet.
Whispers of tales from yesterday,
Metallic clangs of a lady's tray.

The cat takes flight, oh what a sight,
Chasing a shadow with all its might.
Yet that same shadow starts to bite,
Like it's auditioning for a fright night.

A creaky step, a giggle unseen,
Bargains gone wrong at the Halloween scene.
Hide and seek games that turn obscene,
Where curtains flutter in acts of keen.

Oh how they grin through shades of gloom,
Their laughter ripples, it starts to bloom.
With every joke, a touch of doom,
As shadows waltz in the living room.

Songs of the Silent Night

When midnight strikes, the fridge hums loud,
While socks conspire, forming a crowd.
Tunes from the toaster, sung proud,
Join the choir of the couch-bound shroud.

The kettle whistles a jazzy beat,
Each cup joins in with a little feat.
Even the broom finds its own seat,
Dancing along to a playful greet.

Under starlit beams, they prance and sway,
Pretending to work, but they just play.
The moonlight adds to the grand bouquet,
As shadows sing their merry ballet.

In silence, the walls become their stage,
As they learn to laugh, to dance, and engage.
In this quirky tale, they flip the page,
Writing tunes of joy, free from cage.

Portraits in Shadows

On the wall, a shadowy mime,
Strikes a pose like it's showtime.
A top hat, a cane, oh what a climb,
In a world where the absurd can rhyme.

Next to it stands a quirky dog,
With a look that says, 'I'm a fine fog'.
He wags his tail, it's quite a smog,
In a gallery filled with no catalog.

A portrait of cat, with a hat askew,
Rolling its eyes, quite the view.
It pauses, pondering something new,
In this world where the silly grew.

Each shadow dances, tells a tale,
Of mismatched socks and a rubber snail.
They giggle gently, they never pale,
In the gallery where humor sets sail.

The Nature of Echoing Silence

In the garden of quiet, where whispers roam,
Plants wear hats; they call it home.
Worms in bow ties throw a grand dome,
While daisies bloom with friendly foam.

The hedgehog giggles under the sun,
Sipping warm tea, just having fun.
A parade of insects, their own run,
Life's wild party, it's just begun.

A breeze that chuckles, stirs the air,
With secrets brushed in every hair.
The snails glide by, without a care,
Setting the mood, an innocent affair.

The night creeps in, the stars conspire,
With laughter ringing, they never tire.
Every hush holds its own satire,
In the silence where humor takes higher.

Recollections Beneath the Surface

In the attic, there lies a shoe,
Filled with secrets, worn right through.
I tried it on, and what a sight,
It squeaked like mice in the dead of night.

Old photos laugh, with faces aglow,
A cat in a hat—what a strange show!
Grandma's dance moves, a wiggling spree,
As I press rewind, she looks back at me.

The chair creaks softly, a ghostly hum,
That chair, I swear, knows where I'm from.
It rattles stories of all my blunders,
'Twas not my fault'—or so it wonders.

The dust bunnies join in the fun,
As I tell them stories 'til the day is done.
They leap in loops, they wiggle and spin,
In this wild time warp, where do I begin?

Hushed Harmonics of History

In the library, shadows chase books,
They leave behind whispers, playful looks.
A tome falls open to a blank face,
It seems to sigh, 'This is no place!'

The librarian with glasses slips and trips,
Once elegant, now she sends out quips.
Her voice a melody, a quirky tune,
"Library's great, unless you're a raccoon!"

Old clocks tick-tock with a jesting grin,
Saying time's lost, where've you been?
A page flips over like a gossip's tale,
Revealing a secret of a potato sail.

The shelves sing songs, both high and low,
Of misadventures in the melted snow.
So gather 'round, for history's fun,
With laughter and giggles, the day's begun!

Memories Woven into Silence

Beneath the stairs, a curious box,
Filled with letters—oh, what a paradox!
A note from me, in crayon bright,
"Don't eat the cookies, they're an ancient sight!"

A sock puppet greets me with a grin,
It claims it's wise, with a wizard's spin.
"I've seen the world from your foot's strange view,
But was it the left or the one smelly shoe?"

The closet whispers, "Shh, it's a game,"
Clothes hang out, saying, "Who's to blame?"
A tutu sways, like a ballerina's show,
But it's only a coat, what a big throw!

In this quirky realm of woven lore,
Each silence tickles; how could we ask for more?
So let's weave together the laughter and cheer,
For in this quiet, the funny is clear!

A Journey Through the Abyss

Down the hall, a rogue cat prances,
In a world of weirdly funny glances.
Every creak echoes, as if to say,
"Is it night or did we skip the day?"

The fridge hums tunes of culinary dreams,
But all it holds are some old ice creams.
A peanut butter jar, it chuckles and sways,
"It's been a while; let's dance and play!"

The bathroom mirror starts to giggle,
With toothpaste jokes, they always wiggle.
"Do you have a mint? Or maybe a brush?
Let's scrub it out, in a loving rush!"

In this abyss of silly and wild,
Every corner tells tales, as it's reviled.
With laughter echoing, we yawp and glide,
For in this journey, joy is our guide!

Faint Notes from Forgotten Lives

In the corners, laughter flits,
As dust bunnies dance in their skits.
Old shoes tap on a squeaky floor,
While cats plot mischief behind closed doors.

A clock chimes twice, but it's off beat,
Time has a schedule it doesn't repeat.
Forgotten friends in a game of charades,
Play dress-up in the light that parades.

Cupcakes spill from a laughing jar,
Socks worn by knights in a pancake war.
Giggling ghosts and their pastry fights,
Making mornings sparkle with silly bites.

Whimsical tunes from a gramophone,
Where shoes tap dance, yet feel alone.
In the cupboard, the pantry sings,
Of far-off feasts and odd little things.

The Language of Shadows

In the quiet, shadows play their prank,
Conspiracies in the bed of a tank.
The curtains wiggle in giggling fright,
As dishes chip away in delight.

Lampshades whisper secrets untold,
While teapots gossip over stories old.
Bouncing off walls, a silly refrain,
Like cats who think they can sing in the rain.

Socks from the dryer take off on a spree,
In dance-offs with towels, oh don't you see?
Toasters toast in a curious cheer,
While muffins tumble down, never fear!

Dining chairs creak in a stand-up show,
As napkins fold into origami blow.
The dining room hosts a silent parade,
Where laughter's the currency, joy isn't delayed.

Whispers of Yesterday's Light

In the attic, a hat does a jig,
Next to a skateboard playing big.
Yearbook signed by a ghostly hand,
Reading "Be silly! It's perfectly planned!"

A cereal box full of tales to snack,
Crunchy secrets that never look back.
Tiles tap softly with shoes from the past,
Taking a swim in a sea of contrast.

Mirrors laugh at the socks hugging tight,
As the fridge hums a tune late at night.
Puddles of light waltz on wooden floors,
Each one whispering, "Open the doors!"

When windows giggle behind drawn shades,
And chairs spin tales of fantastical raids,
The past plays hopscotch with the present's glow,
Casting shadows of joy in a playful throw.

Chronicles in the Air

Clouds drape stories like blankets tossed,
While laughter leaps, never quite lost.
Breezes carry a faintly off-key tale,
Of paper airplanes that inevitably fail.

Windows flash with winks and grins,
As watching leaves think of where time spins.
Butterflies trade jokes with birds on the run,
Twirl through the air, chasing the sun.

Puppies bark in a mock debate,
Over who gets the last cookie on the plate.
Chasing shadows from new light's glare,
On afternoons that dance without a care.

Voices rise as the sun sinks low,
Stars sweeping in for the evening show.
Moonbeams chuckle with twinkling sighs,
In the chronicles where fun never dies.

Unraveled Threads of the Past

In the attic, dust bunnies play,
Chasing memories, they laugh and sway.
Old sweaters giggle at yesterday's fashion,
While moths waltz in a quirky passion.

Faded photos clamor for a glance,
Each snapshot whispers, ``Oh, what a chance!``
A wild hairstyle from '89,
Makes people chuckle, it's quite divine.

A sandwich wrapped, forgotten in time,
Wants attention, oh what a crime!
It tells of lunches, long draped in shame,
Grew stale and funny, yet feels no blame.

Nostalgia's pranks, with playful delight,
Make shadows dance in the soft moonlight.
With laughter ringing from each old nook,
In this crazy space, memories cook.

Ghosts of Laughter and Tears

The old house creaks with giggles at night,
Chasing away sadness, turning it bright.
It seems the walls have stories to share,
Of silly moments and secret despair.

A chair by the fire spins tales on its own,
Whispering jokes in a comedic tone.
The chandelier sways, dressed up for the fun,
Reminding us all that we're never done.

Footsteps tap in a lively parade,
With every mishap, the laughter cascades.
A vacuum hums in a rhythmic embrace,
Dancing around like it's winning a race.

Through whirlwinds of memories bound in delight,
The past holds a mirror reflecting the light.
Amidst the tears that sometimes appear,
The ghosts of joy linger, so always stay near.

Hushed Secrets in Empty Rooms

Quiet corners share whispers of glee,
Mice tell stories that we can't quite see.
An empty chair spins tales of delight,
Of guests that once feasted far into night.

Curtains flutter with mischievous cheer,
Dust motes dance as if they can hear.
They gather around to listen so close,
To tales of old friendships, laughter, and prose.

Shadows play peek-a-boo under the stairs,
Cracks in the walls hold tales of our cares.
In a closet, a sock sings a silly song,
While a jacket recalls where it has been wrong.

These hush-hush moments, filled to the brim,
With laughter and warmth, never too dim.
In empty rooms where secrets reside,
The joys of the past dance side by side.

Memories Linger Like Faint Breeze

A gentle whisper floats through the air,
Carrying laughter that once filled a chair.
Like a joke told at breakfast, it tickles the mind,
Hitchhiking shadows, both silly and blind.

The scent of cookies from long years ago,
Makes the heart giggle with comfort and glow.
A worn-out rug knows all the old pranks,
Each creaky floorboard, the laughs and the thanks.

Sunlight spills in, teasing the light,
As memories flutter, taking off flight.
A friendly cat, once part of the scene,
Prowls through the stories, keeps everything clean.

In the twilight glow, fun memories tease,
Like a playful breeze that knows how to please.
So we chuckle aloud and soak in the glee,
For those sweet echoes are still wild and free.

A Chorus of Forgotten Dreams

In the attic, dusty tales dance,
Forgotten socks take a chance.
Naps that turned into grand parades,
With tangled hair and lemonade shades.

Louder than laughter, a muffin's sigh,
Where a shoe just spoke with a wink to a pie.
Cupboards sing songs of silly delight,
While the clock laughs at another long night.

Chairs gossip about who sat where,
As the cat critiques every hair.
Tales of trips that never occurred,
To places where no one ever stirred.

A chorus arises from old wooden beams,
Oh, the comedy in forgotten dreams.

Memories at the Threshold

A shoe horned in, right by the door,
Waves goodbye to a mop on the floor.
Doorknobs chuckle, creaky and bright,
As dust bunnies dance in beams of light.

The couch has tales of snacks long gone,
While woolly socks engage in a con.
Pillows argue over who gets the hug,
While Lego bricks form a perfumed rug.

An old umbrella sneezes with glee,
At the thought of a wild, wet spree.
Memories spill, like spilled beans they glide,
As shoes laugh to see the cat take a ride.

At the threshold, laughter does spin,
With each little mishap found within.

Whispers in the Corridor

Down the hall, a whisper flies,
Mixing secrets with awful pies.
Plastered walls hold giggles tight,
As shadows prance in dimming light.

Clocks all tick with synchronized flair,
While forgetful chairs shake their flair.
Socks debate if they'll settle down,
Or throw a party in their small town.

Dust motes twirl in pirouettes grand,
While old games rustle at their command.
Gumy bears shoot for the best punchline,
As whispers roll out a grand design.

In the corridor where jokes abound,
Every corner has laughter profound.

Shadows of Forgotten Dreams

In a room where echoes softly tread,
A vacuum hums, dreaming of bread.
Laundry flails in a contest of grace,
While pants appear to start a race.

A pickle jar winks from its shelf,
Chortling softly to itself.
Curtains sway as they start to groove,
Underneath the disco moves.

Mugs gossip about yesterday's brew,
And how they miss a toddler's chew.
Dust settles like stars in a pot,
In the laughter of what was forgot.

Shadows jiggle with glee in the nooks,
While memories dance like picture books.

The Forgotten Choir

In the dusty corner, they gather round,
With voices that can barely make a sound.
A cat joins in, much to their surprise,
The high notes suddenly turn to meows.

Their songs of woe are out of tune,
While chairs and tables begin to croon.
A laugh escapes from shadows near,
As they perform for the ghostly deer.

One sings of love, the other of cheese,
Each note she swears will bring him to his knees.
But all that lingers in the stale air,
Is a chorus of snickers and a chair's loud creak.

With every misstep and each funny fall,
They seem to relish the joy of it all.
For in this forgotten, quirky choir,
Laughter's the music they truly desire.

Resonance of Old Lament

In the corner, a ghost strums an old guitar,
While the cobwebs sway like they're at the bar.
A tune of heartbreak, but not quite sad,
The shadows dance; it's not so bad.

The chandeliers flicker with disco light,
As memories whimper, trying to take flight.
A joke was told in a somber tone,
Now even the old walls crack a groan.

Lost loves lament with a tickle of glee,
While a banshee makes tea, oh joy, can't you see?
Their tears become giggles, a fun little game,
In this hall of lament, no one feels shame.

Even the clocks can't keep time right,
Ticking backward, singing soft into the night.
Old hearts giggle at stories once grand,
As echoes of laughter drift hand in hand.

Stories Trapped in Silence

Among the books, whispers softly creep,
Tales of mischief that make you leap.
Dust motes dance in sunlit streams,
But silence shares the silliest dreams.

The old armchair has a secret to spill,
Of socks that vanished, oh what a thrill!
It creaks a story of great surprise,
Of snacks left hidden right under your eyes.

A pen rolls off with a chuckle and spin,
Writing tales of troubles we all get in.
Scribbles of laughter fill empty spaces,
While giggles hide behind forgotten faces.

So hush, listen close, the silence is ripe,
With stories that giggle and banter and hype.
In corners where shadows and laughter entwine,
The tales waddle forth, a punchline divine.

Shadows Singing Softly

In the moonlight, shadows sway and twirl,
With whispers of mischief, they frolic and whirl.
Their melodies tickle the edges of night,
As they bicker playfully, a humorous sight.

One shadow trips over an unseen shoe,
While another rolls eyes and giggles too.
With soft little lyrics that twist and bend,
Each laugh a reminder that fun has no end.

The walls take a peek, with painted delight,
As shadows harmonize in the pale moonlight.
A cheeky duet of the lost and the found,
In this grand hallway, laughter knows no bounds.

So join in the ruckus, don't stand so still,
For the shadows are singing; it's a heavenly thrill.
In a dance of delight, let the night carry on,
For laughter and shadows will forever dawn.

Memories that Wander

In the corners, laughs do play,
Ghosts of past, they dance away.
Forgotten socks beneath the bed,
Whisper tales of joy instead.

Cats are plotting, or so I think,
While I sip on my coffee drink.
They meow secrets, tales of fame,
While I wonder who's to blame.

The fridge hums tunes of late-night snacks,
Spilling tales of cheese and cracks.
Old pizza boxes, stacked with flair,
They giggle softly, unaware.

Laughter skips along the walls,
Chasing whispers through the halls.
Silly moments, they collide,
With memories that play and glide.

The Soundtrack of Shadows

A creaky floor sings like a band,
As shadows stretch across the land.
The toaster pops a lively beat,
While crumbs dance around my feet.

Socks in pairs, where could they be?
A sock thief lurking, so I decree!
They plot adventures under the bed,
While I chase thoughts inside my head.

The pantry whispers secrets grand,
Of cookies baked by a ghostly hand.
They giggle softly with a crack,
As I search for that final snack.

Each flicker of light, a secret told,
In the realm of the bold and old.
The shadows bounce, they twist and twine,
Creating a jest that's truly divine.

Conversations with the Void

In the silence, whispers rise,
A talking chair that tells no lies.
It tells of snacks left on a plate,
In a love affair with fate.

The kitchen clock ticks with a wink,
Rushing me just as I blink.
Beneath the sink, a gurgle's sound,
A playful spirit, homeward bound.

The cat confesses with a purr,
Each laugh she hides, a clever blur.
While I ponder life's great scheme,
She plots a nap as if in a dream.

To the walls, I casually talk,
Sharing jokes with the old wood block.
They respond with creaks and sighs,
Chasing laughter through the skies.

Faded Footfalls in Time

Footprints wander without a clue,
In a world where socks are two.
Each step a giggle, lost in air,
As if the floor had a spy affair.

A playful breeze whirls around,
A tumbleweed's merry sound.
It teases curtains, flirts with light,
Inviting sunbeams to take flight.

The dust bunnies whisper their tales,
Of epic journeys and cardboard sails.
Their laughter echoes through the room,
As I dodge the inevitable gloom.

With each beat of the clock, we learn,
Time's a prankster, twist and turn.
So I dance with my fading steps,
Embracing laughter, no regrets.

Secretive Whispers Linger

Sneaky secrets in the night,
They gossip like a flighty kite.
Creaking doors and hidden stalls,
As laughter dances on the walls.

Peeking through a dusty pane,
Who spilled the juice? There's no refrain!
Chairs that squeak with every thought,
Oh, the trouble that we've wrought!

Muffled chuckles, oh so sly,
Like ninjas creeping, oh my, oh my!
In the attic, socks unfurl,
Who knew this place was such a whirl?

Underneath the moon's soft glow,
We plot and scheme, just for show.
With joyful hearts, we sing our tune,
Forever laughing 'neath the moon.

In the Footsteps of Yesterday

Tiptoeing where shadows play,
Hiding memories, come what may.
Funny faces, ghostly grins,
Remind us of our epic sins.

Oh, what mischief from the past,
Turns simple strolls into a blast.
Running shoes now made of dust,
Step lightly, or you might combust!

We find a sock, it must be blue,
Excuse me, did this come from you?
Laughter spins like autumn leaves,
As yesterday quietly deceives.

In every corner, tales unspool,
As we embark on this silly duel.
Let's trip on laughter, miss the beat,
With memories we never cheat.

Tales of the Untold

In bookcases, legends sleep,
Of banana peels and secrets deep.
The tumble here, a faceplant there,
Tell me, who invented this dare?

Stumbling students, giggles abound,
In these halls, we're homeward bound.
Chased by shadows, bright-eyed glee,
Bouncing off the halls like a bee.

Each corner whispers silly plights,
As bubble gum takes flight at nights.
Chalk dust clouds in the schoolyard breeze,
Reckless fun, if you please!

So gather 'round, let stories flow,
Of younger days, where antics grow.
With every laugh, let joy unfold,
In tales so sweet, yet still untold.

Fragments of Sound in Stillness

Whispers hide beneath the floor,
As chuckles bounce from door to door.
Silly songs and quirky rhymes,
Drift like clouds through playful times.

Rustling papers, clattering pens,
Echoing giggles of old friends.
A pencil drops, a chair will squeak,
In silliness, we're never bleak.

The clock ticks loud with every joke,
As laughter's tangled in the smoke.
Silent moments filled with cheer,
A joke recalled, the end is near!

So let this quiet space explode,
With giddy grins and the stories flowed.
In fragments of sound, our hearts entwine,
Creating chaos, oh so fine!

A Tapestry Woven with Silence

In a room filled with dust, a chair squeaks,
A ghost with no shoes, just a pair of sneaks.
A whiff of old cheese, a mysterious scent,
The laughter of echoes that never were meant.

Lurking in corners, where shadows convene,
A cat with a nudge, returns to the scene.
With yarn balls a-rolling, it leaps with a grin,
While the broom in the closet just wishes to win.

Laughter of pictures that hang by the door,
Each frame has a story that makes us roar.
The carpet does giggle as we shuffle across,
Every step tells a tale, never at a loss.

Here in this haven, each creak finds its muse,
An orchestra plays with just a few shoes.
With echoes of nonsense, and giggles that roll,
We weave through the silence, it's good for the soul.

Ripples Through the Old Timber

In the woodwork's grin, a squeaky cheer,
Timber that chuckles from yesteryear.
A mouse in a hat, with a dance on the floor,
Smart as he is, he can't find the door.

The walls whisper softly, 'Why not join in?'
With a tap dance of dust, where the beams do spin.
Traces of laughter from bygone days,
Tickling the rafters in curious ways.

With a twist and a twirl and a lumberjack's call,
A cabinet opens, revealing it all.
Caught in a prank, it's stuck with a grin,
Wondering if it should let the fun begin.

Time stretches and bends in this playful place,
Where echoes of laughter find room to embrace.
Each plank has a pulse, a humorous tale,
As holiday memories set sail in the gale.

The Unseen Presence of Time

In the tick of the clock, a joke waiting still,
With hands moving slower, it bends to our will.
Tickling the seconds, they jump off the wall,
As laughter rolls out like a marbled ball.

Time winks from corners, a jester divine,
Playing tricks on the shadows, a master design.
Each moment a riddle, a playful charade,
Where giggles are layered, like a classic parade.

In the hush of the night, the crickets all sing,
A symphony made of the silliest thing.
They tease the old floorboards with every slight creak,
Bringing joy to the stillness, they giggle and peek.

Days come and go, all dressed up in cheer,
With clocks wearing costumes, it's perfectly clear.
In this space where time flips, folly expands,
The unseen presence of joy demands.

Relics of Sound in Stillness

In the attic's embrace, old records spin,
With each scratch, a memory—a chuckle within.
The old phonograph grooves with a pirouette,
Declaring itself as the best dancer yet.

Socks on the floor play a slide and a shuffle,
As footsteps awaken a hyperactive shuffle.
In the silence, there's laughter that plays hide and seek,
With spoons in the drawer, they clatter and squeak.

Bottles are rattling, a strum on the shelf,
While the chess set conspires to best itself.
In the stillness, a symphony brews,
As laughter springs forth in well-loved reviews.

Forgotten harmonies linger with flair,
While walls hold the secrets, the giggles in air.
A tapestry woven from strangeness and cheer,
In relics of sound, we find joy ever near.

Beneath the Echoing Ceiling

In a room where whispers play,
Pigeons coo in disarray.
Footsteps hurry down the lane,
While a cat plots its next gain.

A wayward sock begins to dance,
With a rhythm that enchants.
The clock hangs low, its hands tick-tock,
Chasing time like it's a rock.

A sandwich talks, it has a voice,
Declaring lunch its favorite choice.
Fried pickles hold a curious chat,
About the meaning of the spat.

Laughter rolls beneath the beams,
As the world unfolds its dreams.
In this house where quirks reside,
Life's delightful, let's decide!

Lullabies of Lost Years

In the attic, dust can sing,
A toy drum starts a merry fling.
Barbies crack a joke or two,
While G.I. Joe just plays it cool.

Old curtains shake with giggles bright,
As shadows dance into the night.
The old clock winks, it knows the score,
Tickling time, who could want more?

That forgotten cake left on the shelf,
Starts talking about its youthful self.
A phrase caught on a creaky floor,
"Who needs a nap when you can snore?"

Each old tale spins a happy yarn,
Wrapped in colors, bright as dawn.
Sing along with past delight,
In the hush of playful night!

Reveries in the Night

When the moon wears shades of fun,
The teddy bears begin to run.
Ghosts tell stories filled with glee,
While squeaky mice sip chamomile tea.

Beneath the stars, a rubber duck,
Quacks about its latest luck.
The broomstick takes a joyful ride,
Through dreams where friendly ghouls reside.

A potato dreams of being fries,
In a world that wears surprise.
With giggles floating on the breeze,
While the stars make jokes with ease.

The night air hums a wacky tune,
As shadows spin beneath the moon.
In this realm of chuckles bright,
Every moment brings delight!

Chasing After Shadows

In the garden, laughter blooms,
As squirrels plot with silly tunes.
A gnome plays hopscotch with the breeze,
While flowers whisper, "Hey, let's tease!"

The shadows run and hide away,
Playing games at end of day.
The sun throws jokes to moonlit skies,
As night returns with playful sighs.

A chicken fluffs its feathers wide,
Saying, "Why not join the ride?"
Each moment drips with joy's pure art,
As laughter weaves from heart to heart.

Beneath the trees, where secrets curl,
Life's a giggle, let it twirl.
In the dusk, let humor win,
As shadows dance, and dreams begin!

The Dance of Invisibility

In the corner, a shadow sways,
Accidental moonwalk, catching rays.
A ghostly jig, with an absent beat,
Tiptoeing softly, then losing their feet.

Whispers of laughter spill from thin air,
Fumbling dancers, without a care.
They twist and twirl in a clumsy glee,
Invisible partners, too shy to see.

Walls giggle softly, as jesters parade,
Bouncing off echoes, unplanned charades.
Each unseen whirl brings a chuckle or two,
As the living room hosts a phantom review.

In corners and nooks, the antics unfold,
Socks go a-dancing, both brave and bold.
With every mishap, a chuckle is born,
Invisibility reigns, but oh, how they twirl!

Chronicles of the Fading

Once lived a man, quite hard to see,
Chasing his thoughts like a runaway flea.
He'd venture through halls, a tumble of flair,
But somehow his presence just wasn't there.

Widgets and gadgets would clatter and clank,
While he raised a toast with an absent prank.
The walls would reply with a raucous cheer,
As he made his rounds, too clever, I fear.

Scavenging joy from the air and the light,
His tales would dissipate, barely in sight.
A laughing ghost in a bustling spree,
Chronicles written by spirits so free.

In corners he lingered, tales half there,
Emerging from shadows to claim his share.
Laughter and stories, his ultimate goal,
Invisibility crafting each comical scroll.

Reverberate through Time's Embrace

In a realm where the clocks play a trick,
Time wears a mustache, oh what a gimmick!
Tick-tocking humor as laughter unfolds,
Each second a punchline, never grows old.

Wobbling walls with a ticklish knack,
Chasing their tails like a well-trained pack.
Belly laughs bounce as the minutes retreat,
Reverberating warmth in this rhythmic beat.

Ghosts of the past throw a quirky dance,
On the floor of nostalgia, they'll prance.
With grand pianos made of jest and delight,
Singing sweet melodies well into the night.

Moments of joy wrapped in giggles and fun,
With time as the jester, all worries undone.
As laughter reverberates in this space,
We find our own rhythm in time's embrace.

The Silent Ballet of Longing

In the quiet of longing, a shuffle appears,
Unseen pirouettes through the halls of our fears.
With a wink and a nod, they glide through the dark,
As whispers of dreams sing a magical lark.

Tiptoeing softly, they're light on their toes,
Clutching at wishes nobody knows.
In the still of the night, they twirl with delight,
Performing a ballet beneath the moonlight.

Missing the chance for a laugh and a cheer,
They dance in the silence, with no one to hear.
Exchanging their tales in a hush and a sigh,
Silent ballet painted against the night sky.

But in all their longing, a secret they keep,
Laughter is buried beneath dreams that leap.
Through shadows they frolic, for all to see,
Longing finds joy in its own jubilee.

Beneath the Surface of Stillness

In a library where silence reigned,
A book sneezed, and everyone feigned.
Pages fluttered, caught in a breeze,
Dust bunnies danced with such ease.

A coffee cup spilled a secret or two,
Muffin crumbs whispered, 'Who knew?'
A pencil fell, made a comic sound,
Laughter erupted, all around.

The clock ticked loud, like a drum in a band,
Even the papers wanted to stand.
Beneath the quiet, a party brewed,
Where mischief and mirth leisurely renewed.

So if you visit, stay for a while,
Let the calmness tickle your smile.
For stillness can have a hilarious bend,
In the nooks where laughter will never end.

Fragmented Histories Float

In the attic where memories crawl,
Old toys giggle and whisper small.
A dusty globe spins tales askew,
While a teddy bear claims he once flew.

A trunk of letters, tangled and old,
Shared secrets of love, half-told.
The past dances in polka dots bright,
Even the shadows burst into light.

Picture frames wobbled, bold and loud,
Grinning at folks who once felt proud.
And somewhere beneath all that mess,
A sock puppet tells of its great success.

So dive deep in this cluttered expanse,
Find laughter in every forgotten chance.
For history's quirks work like a spell,
Transforming the mundane into tales to tell.

Conversations in the Dark

In the dead of night, whispers take flight,
Chairs creak softly, what a delight!
A cat makes a joke, the shadows all laugh,
While the moon plays the part of a curious gaffe.

A sock in the corner begins to debate,
With a rogue post-it who dreams of fate.
Thoughts spill like tea from those who can't sleep,
As secrets of the universe begin to seep.

The fridge hums a tune, a ballad quite grand,
When sporks join in, it's a musical band.
Ideas bounce like popcorn in air,
In the stillness of night, they have not a care.

So if you find yourself up at this hour,
Take heed of the whispers that float like a flower.
For even in darkness, joy finds its way,
With laughter that carries the worries away.

When Time Stands Still

In moments where clocks forget to tick,
A squirrel dances, trying a trick.
The sun and the moon play peek-a-boo,
As shadows comically chase the dew.

An ice cream cone melts, oh what a laugh,
While ants hold a meeting on the sidewalk path.
An old chair creaks with tales from the past,
Where time's lazy dreams are hilariously cast.

Flowers bloom in peculiar hues,
Hummingbirds wonder, which nectar to choose?
Amidst the stillness, butterflies tease,
Tickling the air with whimsical ease.

So relish the moments when time takes a break,
And life plays the jester in a grand, funny wake.
For in the stillness, joy can be found,
In nonsensical laughter, the world spins around.

Whispers of Forgotten Corners

In corners where dust bunnies dwell,
A grumpy old cat starts to yell.
The chairs all creak with tales untold,
As socks whisper secrets, brave and bold.

A lonesome shoe plays peek-a-boo,
Dancing with dust, oh, what's it to do?
Curtains flutter with a knowing grin,
While chips in the paint laugh at old sins.

A broom sweeps dreams hidden away,
While cobwebs spin yarns of yesterday.
The clock ticks slowly, a jester's cue,
As time plays tricks, just like a shoe.

So listen close, don't let it pass,
For laughter's caught in the mirror's glass.
In forgotten corners, joy will abide,
With whispers and giggles tucked deep inside.

Shadows of Lost Conversations

Chairs talk secrets of a bumpy ride,
While tables ponder if they should hide.
A lamp keeps gossip, bright and loud,
As mismatched forks form a quirky crowd.

Oh, the rumors of that half-eaten pie,
Were they rivals or friends? Oh my, oh my!
The walls are eavesdroppers, dressed in white,
As shadows giggle in the soft moonlight.

Once was a cereal that flew to the moon,
It missed, but the spoons sang a silly tune.
A broken chair leg gives a sly wink,
As rumbles of laughter begin to link.

In the echoing space where whispers collide,
Every shadow tells tales they'd confide.
So munch on the sunlight like chips in a bowl,
And listen for laughter, it makes the heart whole.

Distant Footfalls in Memory

In the hallway, footsteps jog and skip,
Chasing the laughter, a wild trip.
An old roller skate hums a tune,
While dust motes dance like balloons in June.

A forgotten ball rolls with a grin,
It knows of the fun that lies within.
The echoes of races, so absurd and wild,
Are bookmarks of joy from the heart of a child.

Each thud and patter spills a tale,
Of hide-and-seek turned epic fail.
The carpet giggles, soft and plush,
As the memories rush in a joyful hush.

So hear this symphony of playful dreams,
A parade of giggles and muffled screams.
In distant footfalls, history calls,
As laughter endures in the maze of the halls.

Murmurs of the Silent Gallery

In the gallery where silence sings,
Pictures chatter about fanciful things.
The sculptures nod with a cheerful cheer,
While the vases gossip, oh-so-clear.

A painting winks, it knows it's grand,
While a brushstroke rebels, feeling unplanned.
The frames hold secrets of times gone by,
With whispers of wishes that reach for the sky.

Old tiles gossip in a patterned dance,
Wondering if the world's given a chance.
Dust motes flutter like butterflies free,
While the benches groan, "Come sit with me!"

So stroll through this gallery, take a peek,
At murmurs of joy that seem to speak.
In the silence that fills the colorful space,
Find laughter and warmth in each friendly face.

Hushed Secrets of the Ages

In shadows where whispers dance and sway,
Old chairs giggle at tales from yesterday.
A sock once lost plays tag with a shoe,
Worn-out stories age like fine brew.

Dust bunnies waltz, in slippers they glide,
While clocks tick on, with nothing to hide.
The pantry's been raided by a band of ants,
Chorusing laughter in vegetable pants.

Faded portraits wink with a knowing grin,
As if to say, 'Let the mischief begin!'
Mirrors chuckle at the fumbles we make,
While old floorboards creak with each silly quake.

Beneath the old stairs, a creature takes flight,
Chasing its tail, oh what a delight!
The tales they spin when no one is near,
Are antics of joy wrapped in dust and cheer.

The Song of Time Passing

Tick-tock goes a clock with a playful smirk,
As time pulls pranks, it's all just a quirk.
It claims to be wise but trips on its feet,
Sending past moments in a comical heat.

Footsteps frolic down a slippery lane,
While toddlers launch pies with triumphant reign.
In the garden, veggies sing out loud,
Chanting melodies that draw a crowd.

A cat catches rays of sun just to nap,
While socks orchestrate an invisible clap.
Time rushes by with a wink and a nod,
But the moments we keep are treasures, how odd!

Like peanut butter fights with the jelly on toast,
Time's just the jester, and we are the host.
So dance in the chaos, let laughter prevail,
For life's silly song is the grandest tale.

Reflections in Dimly Lit Corners

Mirrors in corners are plotting a scheme,
Mimicking faces as they giggle and beam.
A hat exchanges jokes with an old dusty broom,
Creating a ruckus in the dimly lit room.

Footprints of mice map an adventurous night,
While shadows make faces that spark pure delight.
Cobwebs are curtains for shows yet untold,
As dust turns to laughter, and silliness unfolds.

The old armchair sighs in a comical pout,
Craving the company of wanderers about.
Books whisper secrets of wild tales whole,
As lanterns flicker with a mischievous goal.

Each trinket's a witness to hijinks on cue,
Chasing the echoes of moments so true.
In the dim corners where time takes a pause,
Laughter reigns freely, while chaos gives applause.

Sighs of the Unseen

Behind the curtains, there's laughter so bright,
As playful shadows engage in a fight.
A teapot chuckles with every steeped brew,
While spoons and forks dance, in a merry view.

The fridge plays host to a yogurt debate,
On who gets the last slice of cake in fate.
Pantry bears witness to sticky hand glee,
As cookies escape on a daring spree.

A mop tells tales of ballroom affairs,
While brooms sweep up all the silly stares.
In the quietest moments, the giggles still rise,
In every crevice where the whimsy lies.

Lampshades engage in a chat about light,
As pillows form jokes that take off in flight.
The unseen sighs come alive with a cheer,
Reminding us always that laughter is near.

The Imprints of Silence

In shadows where the laughter hides,
A sneeze might echo, humor bides.
The cat's sly grin, it mocks the night,
As socks parade without a fright.

A rogue shoe tumbles, don't you dare,
To trip on fruit that's rolling there.
Banana peels and jokes collide,
In silent rooms, our laughter hides.

When curtains sway, they seem to tease,
While ghosts of giggles float with ease.
A slamming door and startled mice,
Are perfect for a prankish slice.

In corners where old does defend,
The walls will giggle, bend and blend.
With winks and nods from far-off places,
We cling to echoes and their graces.

Soft Calls from Distant Rooms

I hear the echoes of your snack,
A rustling bag, the playful crack.
Your giggles drown my serious plight,
As we indulge till we unite.

A rubber duck is on the run,
While over there, you find the fun.
The tumble of a distant fall,
Is everyone trapped in that big hall?

There's whispers wearing silly hats,
And dogs that dance with shaggy mats.
A giggling ghost in striped pajamas,
Is causing chaos with their dramas.

So here we are, amidst the chaos,
With silly songs that bring the pathos.
We share our laughter, round and bold,
In rooms where whispers weave the old.

Timeless Whispers

Underneath the ancient lamp,
There's a voice with quite the camp.
It speaks of socks lost in the void,
And challenges, your skill deployed.

The clock strikes twelve, it sings with glee,
As a dust bunny rolls to me.
Their laughter tickles, here to stay,
With all the squirrels, they join the play.

In every creak of worn-out wood,
Lies a tale, misunderstood.
The mischievous sprites both hare and tortoise,
Compare their leaps, and it's quite laudous!

Let's dance with whimsy, fly like leaves,
As ancient whispers weave through eves.
In timeless fun, we share our breath,
In all these quirks, there lies no death.

The Unseen Specters Dance

A ghostly jig in the cool moonlight,
Casts shadows twisting, oh so tight.
They pull the curtains, swing the doors,
And steal the snacks, oh what a chore!

They tumble 'round in colorful shoes,
While giggles haunt the midnight blues.
Specters stealthy, join the fun,
As laughter pulls us, one by one.

With every twirl, a tale unfolds,
Of silly mishaps, heroes bold.
They dance through time, in joyful prance,
Encouraging all for a chance to dance.

Upstairs and down, they spin with glee,
In empty rooms, it's just you and me.
So join the revelry, take a chance,
Among unseen friends, let's all dance!

Fragments of Time in the Air

Laughter bounces off the ceiling,
Old jokes still have a nice feeling.
Tickling thoughts dance around,
In every corner, giggles are found.

Memories flutter like old hats,
Sitting on shelves, just like old cats.
They whisper secrets, playful and light,
Making the shadows giggle at night.

Chasing the breeze, we spin and sway,
While dusty old scrolls giggle away.
Time plays tricks with a chuckle and grin,
Leaving us wondering where to begin.

In this whimsical world, we frolic free,
Waltzing with whims, just you and me.
Each breath a joke, each smile a cheer,
Fragments of laughter linger near.

Reflections Against Dusty Walls

Who knew walls had so much to say,
Telling quick tales in a funny way?
With dust bunnies strapped to their sides,
They gleefully giggle while memory hides.

Once a grand party, now just a play,
The echoes of laughter won't go away.
Mirror shards chuckle in their frame,
In this dusty room, they're all still game.

The chair creaks loudly, asks for a dance,
Dusty old shoes still take the chance.
Each little squeak is a punchline dropped,
In this dim lit space, joy never stopped.

Photographs wink from their places high,
Grinning at moments that sneakily fly.
Time might be fractured upon these walls,
Yet silence is filled with hilarious calls.

The Language of Faded Portraits

Staring back at us from the past,
Faded faces with laughter cast.
Each brushstroke hides a little jest,
Smiling through time, they can't resist.

With crooked grins and wild hair,
Brushing off time with casual flair.
Whispers of humor spin in the air,
In the language of giggles; feelings laid bare.

Those painted eyes that twinkle bright,
Mischievous souls in the soft light.
They chuckle softly at our surprise,
As we decipher their laughter in disguise.

Each canvas tells a story grand,
As portraits tease with a wink and a hand.
In rooms filled with colors, we find delight,
Language of joy makes every night bright.

Resonance of these Deserted Spaces

Step inside, hear the giggles rise,
From beanbag chairs and well-placed pies.
These empty rooms hold a carnival,
Memories flutter, alive and carefree, after all.

The squeak of a door is a punchline dropped,
Like a rubber chicken, it's always propped.
Even in silence, there's a light chuckle,
In deserted spaces, joys interlock like a buckle.

A cat naps peacefully on the floor,
Watching shadows play find-and-seek at the door.
With a twitch of its ear, it's in on the fun,
In this playful realm, the laughter's never done.

Each corner hides a funny twist,
A popped balloon or a forgotten list.
In these still spaces, humor finds ways,
To linger and dance through the pastel days.